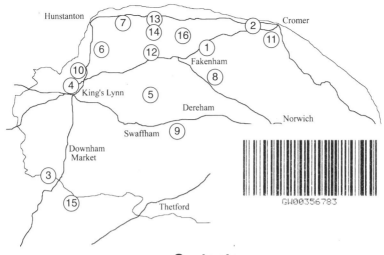

Contents

All map references in this booklet are prefixed with the number of the 1;50,000 Landranger Series of Ordnance Survey maps. The references also apply to the 1;25,000 Explorer series.

1 – Fakenham Town Walk

6 Miles

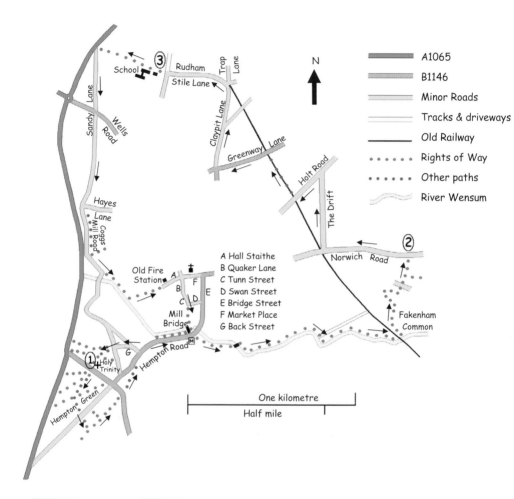

Map labels:

School, ③, Rudham, Stile Lane, Trap Lane, N

Sandy Lane, Wells Road, Claypit Lane

Greenway Lane, Holt Road

Hayes Lane, Mill Road, Coggs Road, The Drift

Old Fire Station, ②, Norwich Road

Mill Bridge, Fakenham Common

①, Holy Trinity, Hempton Road, M, G

Hempton Green

Legend:

▬▬▬	A1065
▬▬▬	B1146
▬▬▬	Minor Roads
——	Tracks & driveways
——	Old Railway
• • • •	Rights of Way
• • • •	Other paths
∿∿	River Wensum

Point labels:

A Hall Staithe
B Quaker Lane
C Tunn Street
D Swan Street
E Bridge Street
F Market Place
G Back Street

One kilometre

Half mile

Fakenham is a busy market town with a good selection of shops, a racecourse and some very attractive open spaces for leisure activities. The Doomsday Book records the population as 150 in 1086, and later in 1250 the town was granted a charter to hold a market. This walk starts at the outskirts of the town on the car park adjacent to the Church of the Holy Trinity, Hempton (OS Ref. 132/913292).

1) From the car park walk towards the A1065 Swaffham Road and keep on the grass path as it bears left around the church and adjacent cottages. Cross the minor tarmac road and keep straight on the grass path ahead. Walk through this attractive meadow on the mown path where there is a wealth of wild flowers in the summer. Keep on straight ahead as far as an Oak tree on the left. Turn left around the tree and, at the main road, cross over to the waymarked path opposite. At a large open space turn left and follow the path, which heads in the direction of the church, to the next tarmac road. Cross the road to a tarmac path and follow this towards the town centre. When the path joins the road keep on the pavement on the right side of the road and follow it to the Gas Museum. The Gas Works were built in 1845 and were responsible for lighting up the whole town. The museum occupies the site of the old works and still has many of the original features in place. Immediately past the museum, turn right into a gravel yard and pick up the riverside walk ahead. This is the River Wensum, rising to the west at Pockthorpe and heading to Pensthorpe, on its way to Norwich and the sea. Follow the river to a bridge and cross over to the other bank and continue along the path. Where the gravel road bears left away from the river, take the grass path which continues along the river bank. Keep on the path, passing the golf course on the other bank, as far as the three arch bridge. Go under the bridge and immediately turn left along a gravel path across Fakenham Common. Follow the winding path to an estate road. Cross over to the path opposite and, where it meets a broad path, carry on ahead to the main road.

2) Cross the road and turn left along the pavement as far as the letterbox and turn right along The Drift. At the end of the road, by the water towers, turn left and at the old railway bridge cross the road and take the steps down to the old railway. Turn right along the old track and at the end of the cutting go up steps to the main road. Turn left along the road to the traffic lights then turn right into Claypit Lane and follow this to Rudham Stile Lane, turn left and continue until it meets open fields.

3) At the High School and the Sports and Fitness Centre the road bears left. Leave the road and take the waymarked path straight ahead. Immediately before the bypass, turn left along a quiet road and follow it to the main road. Cross the road and continue along Sandy Lane. Just past a road on the left signed "Fakenham" turn left on to a footpath running parallel to the road. At the end of the path turn left to rejoin the road. In a short while where the road bears right, keep on ahead along a riverside path. This is an attractive area for families who come here to feed the chickens and ducks always present. Shortly the path leaves the river to the left to pass by the attractive Elizabeth Fitzroy Sensory Garden associated with the nearby residence for the disabled in the old maltings. At the road keep ahead to pass the Old 1911 Fire Station on the left, heading towards the Parish Church dominating the skyline. At this point the walk may be interrupted by a visit to the town for shopping or refreshment. At the edge of the town turn right and follow National Cycleway 1 into Quaker Lane. Turn right into Tunn Street and at the end follow the Cycleway over the Mill Bridge to the main road opposite the Gas Museum. Turn right along the main road passing the entrance of a builders' merchant where there is a board indicating that this was the site of one of Fakenham's Railway Stations. Turn right down Back Street and then keep left alongside some flint cottages to the road. Cross the road and follow the grass path back to the start.

2 - Sheringham and Holt Railway

6½ Miles

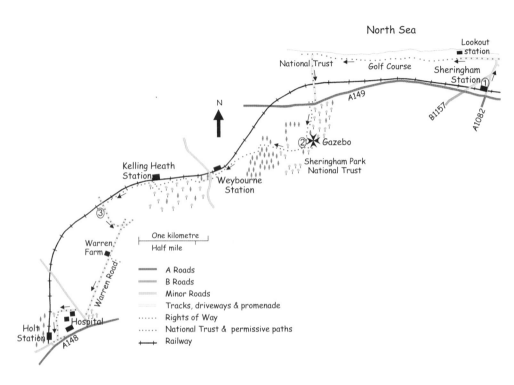

North Sea

Lookout station

National Trust

Golf Course

Sheringham Station ①

A149

B1157

A1082

N

② ✷ Gazebo

Sheringham Park National Trust

Kelling Heath Station

Weybourne Station

③

Warren Farm

Warren Road

One kilometre
Half mile

— A Roads
— B Roads
▦ Minor Roads
═ Tracks, driveways & promenade
⋯ Rights of Way
⋯ National Trust & permissive paths
＋＋＋ Railway

Hospital

Holt Station

A148

Most walks in this book are circular routes mainly because this is a practical way to organise a walk from a car park. Linear walks take a little more organising since there is no car waiting at the end! This can be overcome by using two cars and shuttling, or as in this walk, by using an alternative mode of transport. This day out starts at the Holt Railway Station car park (OS Ref. 133/ 094395) and takes the Poppy Line train to Sheringham Station. The return is a beautiful walk along a section of the coastal path, through parkland and heath, and back to Holt. Users of public transport have the opportunity to travel to Sheringham by normal train, bus or Coasthopper bus, walking to Holt and returning by steam train. For information about the Poppy Line, call 01263 820800; or for "talking timetable", call 01263 820808; alternatively visit *www.nnrailway.co.uk*

1) Leave the platform of Sheringham West Railway Station and turn left along the busy High Street. At the little Market Building carry on straight ahead and follow the street as far as the seaside promenade. Turn left along the promenade and follow this as far as a ramp taking the path to a higher level. Carry on in the same direction, through the gardens and past the boat pond, to go through a gate on to the golf course. There is now a fairly sharp incline to the Watch Lookout Station sitting prominently at the hilltop. Keep on the coastal path alongside the golf course, taking care to avoid the many landslips eroding the cliffs along this area. At the end of the golf course, the route enters the Sheringham Park National Trust property. By the National Trust sign, turn left and follow the track over the railway bridge to the Weybourne road. Turn right along the field-edge path, and in a short distance, turn left to cross the road and enter the park. Take the path straight ahead and walk between the woods and the open fields as far as the Gazebo. Time and energy permitting it is well worth climbing the Gazebo for a view of the surrounding area from above the treetops. Just past the Gazebo, turn right along a path signposted Weybourne.

2) This pretty path wanders along the margin of the woods and open countryside, eventually coming close to the railway near a cutting. Just past the cutting keep right and go through a gate to follow a path to Weybourne Station. At about halfway through the walk, the station is a useful stopping place as it has toilets, café and seats for picnics. To continue the walk, stay on the south side of the station and leave by the car park on to the tarmac road. Take the footpath immediately opposite the car park entrance. The yellow waymark high up a telegraph pole is easily missed. Walk along the gravel drive between houses and keep to the path as it soon runs close to the railway line. Go up the slope to the small platform of Kelling Heath Park Station. This is a request stop for the holidaymakers from the large caravan park on Kelling Heath, which is just a short distance up the hill on the left. From the platform carry on alongside the railway eventually walking above the line as it passes through a cutting. At the end of the cutting there is a level crossing with obvious white gates. Turn left along the broad track across Kelling Heath.

3) Kelling Heath is a Site of Special Scientific Interest, indicating that it is considered to be important as a refuge for wildlife. The dominant plant is the gorse, the flowers of which provide nectar for butterflies. The old saying: "When the gorse is in bloom, it's the season for love" is a reference to the fact that the gorse blooms throughout the year! Walk through the gorse as far as the edge of the caravan park. At the edge of the park, take a small path on the right, signed by the site with a squirrel, to meet the main public footpath. Turn right along this very straight path and follow it, past Warren Farm, as far as the tarmac road. It is possible to turn left here and return to the station via the main A148. However this is a busy road and it is safer to take an alternative route, especially with a large group of walkers. Turn right and, after the houses on the left, turn left along a field-edge track. At the end of the first field take a narrow path through the woods on the left into the hospital car park. Turn right and follow the exit signs to the road. Turn right to return to the station car park.

3 - Downham VCs Remembered

6½ Miles

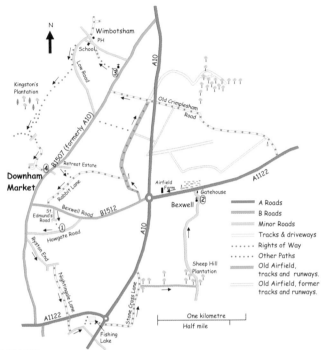

© "Ordnance Survey" 100033886

Early in the second world war the capacity for Bomber Command at Marham was insufficient so a satellite was built to the north east of Downham Market. The Airfield opened in July 1942 with 218 Squadron of Stirling Bombers, later replaced by Lancasters. On the night of August 12/13 1943, Flight Sergeant Arthur Aaron died whilst trying to land a crippled plane in North Africa. He was awarded a Posthumous Victoria Cross. A year later on the night of August 4 1944, Squadron Leader Ian Bazalgette of 635 Squadron died heroically on a sortie to France. He was also awarded a Posthumous Victoria Cross. To date 1,357 Victoria Crosses have been awarded since its introduction in 1857 so it is remarkable that two of these were awarded to airmen of Downham Airfield.

This walk starts at the Howgate car park (OS Ref. 143/615030), walks over the former airfield (now bisected by the A10 bypass) and visits the VC Memorial at Bexwell Church.

1) Leave the car park and turn left towards the town centre. At the main road, turn left and almost immediately left again along Ryston End. Pass Downham Market College on the left, and at the next road junction turn left. Shortly turn right along Nightingale Lane following the sign for National Cycleway 11. Where the main track bears left keep on along a grassy path. Cross the main road by the footbridge and keep straight ahead. At a road junction go ahead between concrete bollards on to a tarmac road. Turn left along the road, and where it bears to the right, keep on straight ahead on to a grass path heading towards the fishing lakes. Almost immediately turn right along a grass path running parallel to the hedge. Cross over the A10 with care and follow the green lane ahead. The path bears to the left through an avenue of trees. Look for a concrete path on the right which appears to be flooded and heading for a large soil heap! Take this path, which is a remnant of the old airfield, and follow it to the road at Sheep Hill Plantation. Turn left and follow the road to Bexwell church.

2) The VC Memorial is situated on the grass in front of the church and it describes the heroics of the two pilots and shows replicas of their medals. Continue along the road passing the large barn-like gatehouse on the right, probably the late 15th-century entrance to Bexwell Hall. Cross over the A1122 and turn left along the footpath to the A10 roundabout. Cross the A10 and continue towards the town centre. Immediately before the first house, turn right along a track, heading for a large communication mast. The track is a remnant of the old airfield. Shortly bear right on to a very wide track, formally one of the main runways. The runway stops at the old Crimplesham Road which, during the war, was closed as it bisected the

airfield. The road was closed once more when the old runways were dug up to provide ballast for the new bypass. Turn left along the old road and then right along the B1507 to Wimbotsham church.

3) Turn left along a path leaving the church to the right. A visit to the church is worthwhile if only to admire the beautifully carved animals on the pew ends. Go through a gate, across a grass field, and leave by another gate on to a road. Carry on along the road to the village centre and bear left around the school with the Chequers Inn across the green on the right. Turn left along Low Road and at the end of the houses on the right go through a gap in the hedge and follow the path inside the hedge to avoid the traffic on this narrow lane. At a concrete pad, turn right along a grass path, heading for the left of Kingston's Plantation. At the end of the wood keep right where the path forks, cross a footbridge and turn left at the end of the path. Cross over the road and continue along the path ahead. At the playing field keep right on to the tarmac road. At the crossroads turn left to the King's Lynn road.

4) Turn left along the road and take the second road on the right (Retreat Estate). Turn right again and at a play area cross diagonally to a path in the far corner. At the end turn right along an open grass area and cross the next road continuing along the path. At the end of Rabbit Lane turn left and then right into St Edmund's Road. Turn left into St Edmund's Terrace and then immediately right on to the Howgate playing field. Cross the field to return to the start.

4 - King's Lynn and West Lynn Ferry

7 Miles

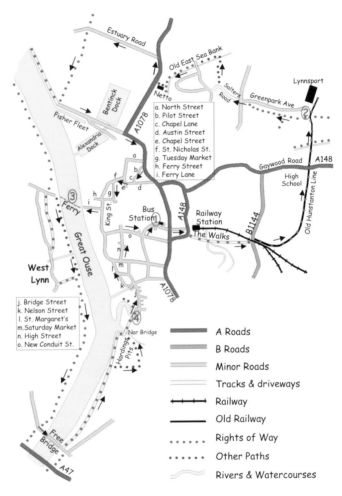

Estuary Road
Old East Sea Bank
Lynnsport
Netto
Salters Road
Greenpark Ave
Bentinck Dock
Fisher Fleet
Alexandria Dock
A1078

a. North Street
b. Pilot Street
c. Chapel Lane
d. Austin Street
e. Chapel Street
f. St. Nicholas St.
g. Tuesday Market
h. Ferry Street
i. Ferry Lane

Gaywood Road
A148
High School
Old Hunstanton Line

③ Ferry
King St.
Bus Station
A148
Railway Station
The Walks
B1144

West Lynn

Great Ouse

j. Bridge Street
k. Nelson Street
l. St. Margaret's
m. Saturday Market
n. High Street
o. New Conduit St.

Nar Bridge
A1078

④

Hardings Pits

Free Bridge
A47

	A Roads
	B Roads
	Minor Roads
	Tracks & driveways
	Railway
	Old Railway
	Rights of Way
	Other Paths
	Rivers & Watercourses

This route is designed for walkers who prefer to use public transport to get to the starting point. It starts at Lynn bus station (OS Ref. 32/621201) and passes the railway station almost immediately. There are free car parks at Lynnsport and West Lynn side of the ferry. Along the route there are glimpses of Lynn's development from the old town buildings to the Fisher Fleet to the modern industrial estates and shops and a view of the new paper mill.

1) Leave the bus station by the main road into the station. Pass the Lord Kelvin pub and cross over the main road down Waterloo Street to the railway station. Turn right in front of the station and in about 100 yards turn left into the Walks. At the end of the Walks, turn left over the level crossing and immediately right along the Old Hunstanton Line. At the path junction follow the signs to Lynnsport. Pass King Edward VII High School, on the left, cross Gaywood Road and continue along the old railway to Lynnsport.

2) Immediately before the car park, turn left along a tarmac path to eventually join Greenpark Avenue. Turn left and cross the next road into the unmade Salters Road. Where the road bears left, take the grass path on the right, heading for a footbridge in the far right corner. Cross the bridge and turn left along Old East Sea Bank. Cross over the next road and, immediately after passing a footbridge on the left, turn right past Netto to the Dock Road. Turn right and keep to the pavement to the traffic lights. Cross by the lights and carry on straight ahead along Estuary Road. Turn left at the Pink House along a grass footpath. A dip in the path indicates that at one time trains carried raw materials into the Dow Factory. At the end of the path carry on ahead to the Fisher Fleet. Turn left alongside the moored boats landing their catch on to the jetty. At the main road, keep to the pavement on the right and cross North Street. In about 50 yards, turn right along a narrow passage into Pilot Street. Follow this cobbled street past St Nicholas Chapel and bear left into the still cobbled Chapel Lane. Turn right into Austin Street and cross over Chapel Street into the car park

opposite. Leave the car park by the far right corner and turn left to Tuesday Market. Follow around the market clockwise to the opposite corner by the Globe Hotel. Turn left into King Street and in about 100 yards follow the signs to the ferry on the right.

3) Take the ferry to West Lynn. The ferry runs every 20 minutes except Sundays and Bank Holidays, and the fare is 70p. After leaving the ferry by the ramp, turn left along the long boardwalk. Follow the river bank to the Free Bridge. Turn left over the bridge and immediately left back along the river bank. At the first wooden carving, turn right into Hardings Pits and wander around this area admiring the carvings. Eventually rejoin the main path by the Nar Bridge.

4) At the tarmac road, turn left past the remains of the Greyfriars and carry on to Bridge Street. Pass the Greenland Fishery building on the left, reputed to be the oldest building in Lynn. Cross the main road and in a short distance turn left into Nelson Street. Carry on to arrive in Saturday Market Place with St Margaret's Church on the right and the Town Hall straight ahead. Turn right across the market and then left along the High Street. At a large tree, turn right along New Conduit Street and then left and right around Westgate Store to return to the bus station.

5 - Brisley and East Bilney

7 Miles

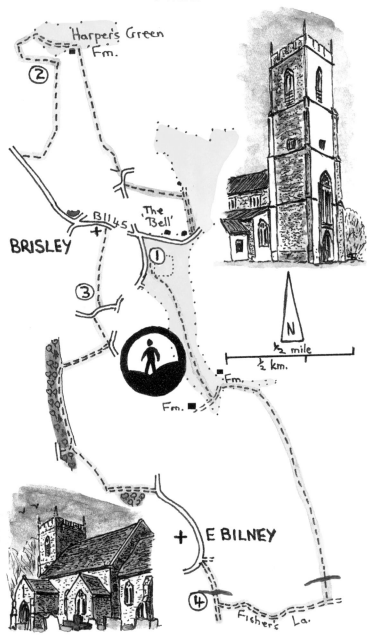

Harper's Green Fm.

②

BII45

BRISLEY

The 'Bell'

①

③

N

½ mile
½ km.

Fm.

Fm.

+ E BILNEY

④

Fisher's La.

Brisley Green is said to be the largest unfenced area of common land in Europe. Until November 2005 access to the 170 acres of common was restricted to residents of the parish and their guests. The CRoW Act of 2000 granted access to all registered common land subject to certain provisions relating to conservation and wildlife. Now it is possible to incorporate access to the common as part of a circular walk around the parish. This walk combines a short circuit to the north of Brisley with a longer circuit around the hamlet of East Bilney. The walk starts at the entrance to the cricket field on the common just a short distance south of the B1145 and just east of the Bell Inn. (OS Ref. 132/955213).

1) From the cricket field walk up to the main road and turn right past the Bell at Brisley to a concrete first world war pillbox. Turn left along a track at the edge of the green, and turn left across a stile just before the first cottage. Keep to the right of the field, cross the stile in the corner, and cross the next field to meet a tarmac road. Turn right along the road for a short way and, where the road bears right, carry on straight ahead along a grass path. Keep to the right at the first junction and then follow the waymarked path straight ahead as far as Harper's Green Farm buildings. Turn left around the farm buildings and follow the farm road to an opening on the left just past the entrance to a gas installation. Take the path past a pond to a stile into a grass field on the left. Cross the field almost back to the farm and then turn right along a field edge path.

2) Follow the path across fields and around some houses to the road. Turn left along the road to the main B1145. Turn left to Brisley Church. The large Church of St Bartholomew is normally open and well worth a visit. It was built over a period between 1347 and 1450 and has features that indicate that it was designed by a number of architects working on other Norfolk churches during that period. The coloured bosses on the nave roof, the remains of the painted walls and the stained glass of the east window are among the more notable points of interest. Carry on along the road to the end of the churchyard and take a path on the right between the village sign and a telephone box. Go through the hedge and then turn right along the field edge.

3) Just before the end of the field, by two large oak trees, the path crosses to the other side of the hedge. At the road turn right for a few yards and then left across the next field heading for a large tree. At the tree turn right along a broad track and follow this to the wood. Turn left along a path running just inside the wood. Although this area is known as Bilney Common it does not come under the free access land legislation. The act only applies to "registered commons". All "commons" have owners. Originally the commons belonged to the Manor and certain "commoners" had rights to graze animals or collect wood and so on from the common in exchange for services rendered to the Lord. Over time many commons were taken back into the hands of the Lord of the Manor, and the commoners either lost their rights or exchanged them for money or a parcel of land. In the 1940s a register was opened to record the rights of the remaining commoners and only commons registered at this time are included in the access legislation.

About 100 yards before a tarmac road turn left through a metal gate and follow the waymarked path to a black shed and builder's yard. Leave the shed to the left and then turn right along a field edge path. At a cross path turn left through a wood. At the next road turn right to pass East Bilney Church on the right. Unfortunately this pretty flint church is locked and there is no indication of a key holder. Just past the church the road bears right. At this point take the track straight ahead called Folly Lane. There is a large house in the trees on the left. The folly perhaps?

4) Cross the Black Water by a footbridge by a ford and shortly turn left along Fisher's Lane. Both of these lanes appear on the maps as white roads and sometimes it is difficult to establish the presence or absence of a right of way along these lanes. In this case a request to the County Council footpath officer established the right of way. At a cross path turn left to cross the Black Water again and carry on along this path for almost a mile to a gate. Go over a footbridge and through the gate into a water meadow. Keep to the left hedge as far as the far hedge and then cross the field to the right to a stile. Cross over the stile and bear left across the common between the two farms and pick up the farm road across the common. From this point make your way across the common at any convenient point to return to the start.

6 - Sedgeford and Snettisham

7¹/₂ Miles

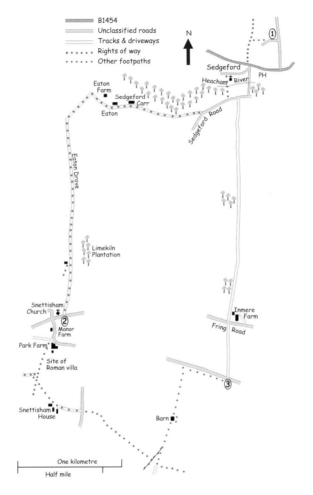

▓▓▓	B1454
▓▓▓	Unclassified roads
	Tracks & driveways
• • • • •	Rights of way
• • • • •	Other footpaths

N ↑

Sedgeford

Eaton Farm

Sedgeford Carr

Eaton

Heacham River

PH

①

Sedgeford Road

Eaton Drove

Limekiln Plantation

Snettisham Church

②

Manor Farm

Park Farm

Site of Roman villa

Snettisham House

Barn

Inmere Farm

Fring Road

③

One kilometre

Half mile

This walk is very much in High Norfolk! The flat areas of The Wash and the Fens have been replaced by gently rolling hills, reaching in places the heady heights of 60 to 70 metres. The villages are in the valleys, with Sedgeford in the valley of the Heacham River, and Snettisham in the Ingold Valley. Much of the walk is over bridleways and broad farm tracks, an indication that this is also riding and shooting country. With the increase in farm mechanisation, many of the old farm buildings are no longer of use. Along the length of this walk there are numerous examples of derelict and ruined farm buildings and a few conversions of old buildings into modern, desirable residences. Start the walk from Sedgeford Village Hall (OS Ref. 132/711368). The village hall is signposted from the centre of the village 250 yards along the Ringstead Road and left along Jarvie Close.

1) Go into the Village Hall car park and turn left across the playing field heading for a gap in the hedge in the far-left corner. Turn left along the footpath to the main road then turn left and almost immediately right towards Snettisham, and then almost immediately right again towards Sedgeford Church. The Church of St Mary the Virgin is one of only 181 round tower churches in England of which 126 are in Norfolk. Many churches with round towers were built in Saxon times but Sedgeford is probably from a later date. The round format enabled the builders to use local flint without the need for expensive Barnack stone for the corners. Immediately past the churchyard, turn left along a narrow footpath. Cross the Heacham river and carry on to the road. Turn right and 250 yards later on, where the road bears left, take the green bridleway on your right. Pass derelict barns on the right and later Eaton Farm, also on the right. The path, Eaton Drove, rises gently and then starts to descend towards Snettisham. Eventually the path joins the road close to Snettisham Church.

2) Turn right along the road to the crossroads. Snettisham Church stands proud with its magnificent stone spire visible for miles around. "Snetesham" is mentioned in the Domesday Book. The present church dates from 1340 but there is evidence of a much earlier church on the site. The Roman villa nearby at Park Farm was considered to be the Roman equivalent of a motorway service station refreshing travellers on their way to the north. From the crossroads turn left towards Park Farm and 200 yards later on turn half right across a grass triangle and through an iron kissing-gate into the fields of Park Farm visitor centre. Continue straight ahead, walking through and alongside the various breeds of sheep and goats and other assorted animals. After the last gate keep straight ahead along the farm track and follow this as it bears round to the left. By Snettisham House the path leaves the main track and follows a narrow track between hedges to the right. Eventually the path joins the main drive and follows this to the road. Cross the road and take the bridleway ahead then follow this for about half a mile to a point where overhead electric cables cross the track. Turn left and take the permissive path to a derelict barn. Detour around the barn and continue in the same direction to the road. Turn right along the headland path parallel to the road to a gap in the hedge.

3) Turn left through the gap, cross the road and then carry on along the stony track ahead. At Fring Road cross over and continue along the Inmere Farm road. This farm is also mainly derelict, the buildings having yielded their pantiles to other developments.   The track is now straight for about one-and-a-quarter miles to the Sedgeford Road. At the road turn right and follow the road around to   the left. The area to the right of the road is the site of the Sedgeford dig. Each summer a group of local archaeologists has excavated this area and   made discoveries of much earlier civilisations. Cross the river and turn right at the road junction. A short distance past the King William pub, turn left along Ringstead Road and then left again into Jarvie Close to return to the start.

7 – Holme and Thornham

7³/₄ Miles

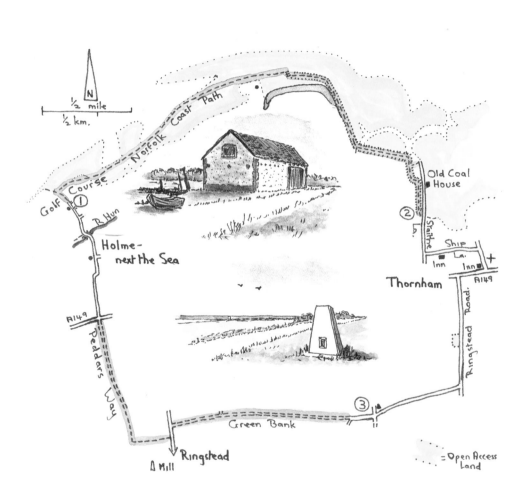

½ mile
½ km.

N

Norfolk Coast Path

Golf Course

R. Hun

① Holme-next the Sea

A149

Peddars Way

Old Coal House

② Staithe

Ship La.

Inn   Inn

Thornham

A149

Ringstead Road

③

Green Bank

Ringstead

△ Mill

⋯⋯ = Open Access Land

Norfolk is fortunate in having two National Trails in the county. The 47 mile long Peddars Way runs roughly north across the county from Knettishall Heath to the coast, and the Norfolk Coast Path runs along the north coast for 46 miles from Hunstanton to Cromer. This walk starts at the meeting point of the two paths at Holme-next-the-Sea and includes parts of both paths. Start from the car park next to the dunes and golf course. (OS Ref. 132/697439.)

1) Leave the car park and turn right across the golf course. At the far side of the course turn right and pick up the well-signed coastal path. For the next two miles there is no need for instructions except follow the clear coastal path. For much of the way there is a boardwalk or a gravel path to encourage walkers to keep off the dunes. Most of these two miles is through an area of open access land that is also a nature reserve. Walkers may of course walk over any of this open access land but, unless there are compelling reasons to do otherwise, it is suggested that the sensitive dunes are left undisturbed as far as possible. The path passes by The Firs, the centre for the Norfolk Wildlife Trust, and the Holme Bird Observatory run by the Norfolk Ornithologists' Association. Both of these are excluded from the Open Access area. The former because the legislation specifically excludes land within 20 metres of a house or building, the latter because it has obtained specific exemption due to the scientific work being carried out with the ringing of birds. Keep on the coastal path until it meets Staithe Lane, Thornham, close to the solitary flint building that is the Old Coal House. This is a reminder that before the days of the motor vehicle much of the traffic was carried by sea. Ships of up to a hundred tons could dock here at Thornham.

2) Leave the Coastal Path for a short distance and carry on along Staithe Lane and turn left along Ship Lane to pass by The Lifeboat Inn. At the end of the lane note some old cottages opposite the junction. Some of these are traditional flint painted white and others are clunch built of white limestone. The latter have small stones set in the mortar layer.

Tradition is that before a witch can enter a house she must first count all of the stones in the building. If she fails before sunrise she is denied entry. Turn right along the road to pass the beautiful building of the 17th century manor house on the right. To the left is the 14th century Church of All Saints, Thornham. If time allows, a visit to the Church to see the 500-year-old rood screen and the octagonal font is well worth while. At the road junction turn right past the Old King's Head, now renamed The Orange Tree, and continue as far as the Ringstead Road on the left. Turn along the Ringstead road and steadily climb towards Beacon Hill. Three quarters of a mile later turn right along the tarmac road as far as a trig point at the next road junction. Trig points were built by the Ordnance Survey as permanent reference points in the triangulation of the country for map making. They have been rendered obsolete now by satellite navigation but remain as permanent reminders of the old system.

3) Continue along the road ahead and, where the road bears left, keep on ahead along the grassy green bank. From this track there are beautiful views across the coastal strip and The Wash, with Skegness visible on a clear day. Carry on along the lane as far as the tarmac road. Turn left for a short distance and then right to join the Peddars Way along a field edge path. To the left is the stock of an old windmill that would have made the most of the wind on this slight rise in the land. Keep on the path to the main road. Cross the road and carry on ahead along Beach Road. At the next junction keep on straight-ahead and cross over the bridge over the River Hun to return to the start.

8 - Colkirk and Oxwick

7³/₄ Miles

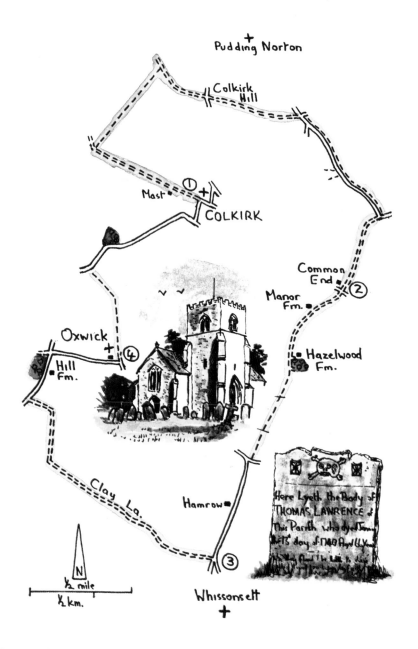

Pudding Norton

Colkirk Hill

Mast

① COLKIRK

Common End

② Manor Fm.

Oxwick

Hill Fm.

④

Hazelwood Fm.

Clay La.

Hamrow

Here Lyeth the Body of THOMAS LAWRENCE of This Parish who dyed ... day of ...

③

N
½ mile
½ km.

Whissonsett

The village of Colkirk, about two miles south of Fakenham, is mentioned in the Domesday Book of 1086 as having a church. Obviously the church was very important since "Kirk" means "church" in both Old English and the Scandinavian languages. Who "Col" was is not clear. What is clear is that in the 17th century there was a thriving community still using the open field system of farming with each villager tending a number of strips in the fields. Like nearby Swaffham, the village once had a "Campingland". The name "Camping" was a dangerous form of football that had to be banned because of the number of injuries caused during the game. This month's walk starts at the village hall car park just on the west side of the churchyard (OS Ref. 132/917265).

1) Walk out of the car park and turn right along a farm track heading for a tall communication mast. At 80 metres this is a high point for Norfolk! There are some good views of Fakenham to the north. Pass the mast on the left and continue along this track for about half a mile. Where the path bears right slightly take the field edge path on the right. Ahead are the village, ruined church and hall of the quaintly named Pudding Norton. Pudding Norton was once a thriving, medieval village but, like many Norfolk villages, it became deserted as the needs of agriculture diminished and the villagers moved into the towns. At the end of the field take the path on the right and follow this to the road at Colkirk Hill. Cross over the road and continue straight ahead on the grass path as far as the crossroads. Cross the road and enter the field on the right. Follow the field headland path alongside the Dereham Road for a little more than half a mile to the point where the path and road bear left. Cross over the road and take the signposted green lane to the right.

2) At a tarmac road by a cottage at Common End cross over and take the concrete road towards Manor Farm. Pass Manor Farm on the right and Hazelwood Farm on the left. Immediately past Hazelwood Farm the farm road bears left. Leave the road at this point and carry on straight ahead over three cross-field paths following the waymarked route. Leave the third field by an opening and bridge over the ditch. Turn right along a tarmac road and a few yards later turn left along the Whissonsett Road. To the right is an orchard as shown on the Ordnance Survey maps but the orchard shown to the left has disappeared. Where the road forks leave the tarmac road and turn right along Clay Lane. (There is a Millennium Seat by the turning that is a useful lunch stop!)

3) Follow Clay Lane for just over a mile until it meets a busy road. Turn right along the road taking great care, as the traffic is fast and sighting not very good. Pass Hill Farm and take the next turn to the right signposted to Oxwick. At Church Cottage, where the road bears right, turn left along a green lane and keep ahead towards Oxwick Church. On the left a path leads into the churchyard and the ruined church. The Church of All Saints dates back to 1300 but, like so many churches in the area, was abandoned in 1940 when the congregation was never more than three. A headstone in the churchyard indicates that a soldier was buried here in 1918 and his grave obviously is visited, as there are Poppy Day Crosses alongside the grave. Further along the graveyard is an interesting tombstone depicting a skull and crossbones. The tablet reads: "Here lyeth the Body of Thomas Lawrence of this parish who died January the 13th day of 1748 aged 66 years." Perhaps at that time the skull and crossbones was a symbol of death rather than having its more recent pirate association?

4) From the church carry on along the grassy path as far as the tarmac road. Turn right along the road and follow it back into the village. Turn left immediately on entering the village and follow the road to the church. The 12th century church is built on the site of a much earlier structure, possibly predating the Norman Conquest. Normally the church is open and visitors will find a descriptive leaflet inside it outlining its long and varied history. Carry on past the church to return to the start.

9 - Holme Hale and North Pickenham

8 Miles

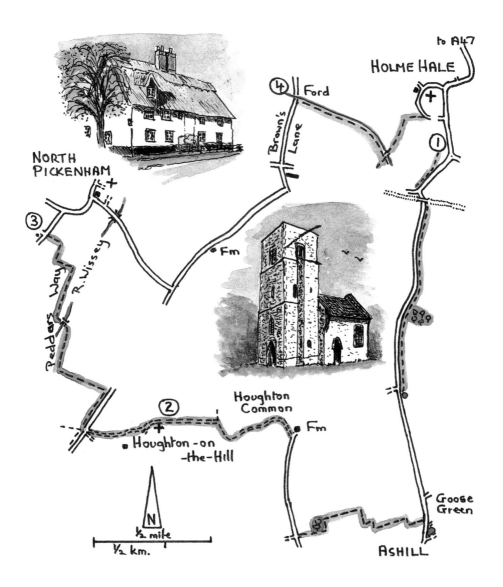

What makes an eight-mile walk into a really memorable ramble? How about good paths that are well signed, co-operative landowners allowing permissive access across their land, great views, something special to visit on the way, and a pub to refresh the weary traveller? This walk takes in the beautiful Church of Saint Mary, Houghton on the Hill, and passes by the Blue Lion at North Pickenham, one of the regular stopping places for those walking the length of the Peddars Way. All of the paths are easy to use and there are excellent views of the surrounding countryside for most of the journey. The walk starts at the Holme Hale Pavilion on the junction of the North Pickenham Road and the Hale Road (OS Ref. 144/889071).

1) From the Pavilion car park cross the playing field to the opposite corner and turn right along a grass field edge path. Immediately there are views of the two turbines, the church and the water tower at Swaffham, and the church at Necton. Leave the field to go left on to the Ashill Road and through the disused railway bridge. Once through the bridge, follow the road using the stewardship path just inside the hedge on the left; stay on this until it runs out then continue along the road into Ashill village. Pass the houses on the left as far as the large, open space of Goose Green. Take the footpath on the right, opposite the Green, signposted between The Old Bakery and Seymore Cottage. Follow the clear path along field edges as far as a tarmac road. Turn right along the road to the farm at Houghton Common. Houghton means "High Place" and again the views from here are spectacular. The later naming of the village "Houghton on the Hill" is therefore tautology, a not infrequent occurrence in place names. Carry on straight ahead on to a green lane that bears left and continues along field edges to an unsigned, large gap in the hedge on the left. Take this green lane as far as the ruins of St Mary's Church. The medieval village of Houghton on the Hill has disappeared long since. Is the 10 yard wide, green lane a clue to its disappearance? This was the width of many droves left between fields during the inclosures of the 18th and early 19th centuries. "Inclosure" meant that the landowner changed his farming from the open strip system to sheep farming. The result

was the loss of employment for many and the subsequent loss of many small villages.

2) Much has been written about the discovery of this ruined church of St Mary by Bob Davy and the effort he has put into its restoration over the past 14 years. Without his intervention, one of the finest examples of a medieval, painted church may have been demolished and lost forever. This site has been, in turn, a Stone Age flint works, an Iron Age settlement, a Roman villa and a ruin used for devil worship. To see the interior of the church it is necessary to telephone Bob on 01760 440470 and make prior arrangements. However, if you do turn up unexpectedly, the chances are that he will be working somewhere around the church and will be happy to show you around. After visiting the church, continue along the lane to the tarmac road. Immediately opposite the lane is a footpath leading to Houghton Springs, a pleasant spot to picnic or watch birds on the lakes. The walk does not include this diversion but turns right along the lane and then left along a field edge to follow the Peddars Way. Follow the well waymarked route across fields to meet a tarmac road at the edge of North Pickenham village.

3) On the opposite side of the road at this point is a memorial to the Men of the USAAF who flew from North Pickenham Airfield in1944 and 1945. Turn right along the road and right at the T-junction to the Blue Lion Inn. In front of the pub turn right again and walk along Houghton Lane to the next road junction. Turn left along the next road and follow this for a little over half a mile to the site of Holme Hale railway station, now converted into a home but still retaining many of the features of the former station. Shortly past the station cross over the main road and follow Brown's Lane to a ford.

4) Just before the ford turn right along a permissive path. Just under half a mile later turn left at a cross path, go over a footbridge and follow the path to the road in the village. Turn left along the road and follow it round to the right to Holme Hale Church and a pretty, thatched cottage. Keep walking ahead to the next road. Turn right and then follow the road back to the starting point.

10 - Castle Rising and Roydon Common

8 Miles

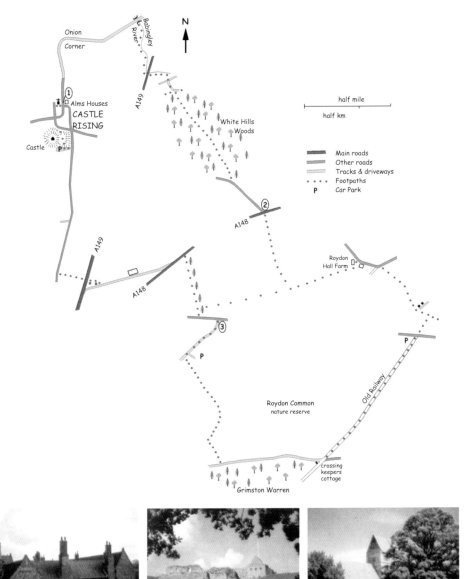

N

Onion Corner

Babingley River

① Alms Houses

CASTLE RISING

A149

White Hills Woods

Castle P

half mile

half km

Main roads
Other roads
Tracks & driveways
· · · Footpaths
P   Car Park

②

A148

A149

A148

Roydon Hall Farm

③

P

P

P

Roydon Common
nature reserve

Old Railway

crossing keepers cottage

Grimston Warren

Where in Norfolk is it possible to find a castle fit for a Queen, a parliamentary borough returning the diarist Samuel Pepys and Britain's first Prime Minister Robert Walpole and his son, Horace, as MPs, and a place that once boasted a seaport greater than King's Lynn's? The answer is in Castle Rising, bypassed by the A149, which once took all the traffic between King's Lynn and Hunstanton through what today is a rather small village. This walk starts from the Old Hunstanton Road between Castle Rising Church and the Alms Houses, now a no- through road. (OS Ref 132/677249).

1) With the Church to your left and the Alms Houses to your right, walk along the Old Hunstanton Road. Go through a gate and then continue along the road. This bears right at "Onion Corner", so called because of the wild garlic which grows in the woods there. Turn right on to a footpath immediately before the bridge over the Babingley River. Follow the footpath, with the river to your left, as far as the A149. This stretch of the river is home to kingfishers that occasionally may be seen as flashes of iridescent blue across the water. Cross the road with care and continue along the riverside path opposite. At the end of the field cross the stile and turn right along the wood's edge. Join the gravel drive and carry on for a while past some houses as far as the end of the garden of the last house. Turn right into the woods and take the left of the two signed paths ahead. Walk through White Hills Woods to the stile and then turn left along the minor road as far as the main A148 ahead.

2) Cross the road and take the footpath opposite. At a track junction, turn left keeping the hedge to your right. At the end of the path, at Roydon Hall Farms, turn left and a few yards later turn right along the minor road. Where Church Lane bears left, keep on straight ahead along a grass footpath following the line of the overhead cables. At the group of houses go through the gate opposite the house to the left of the path. The path heads left across the common. Just before a gate ahead follow the path to the right then keep on this path to a stile by a tarmac road. Cross the road and join the path opposite following the line of an old railway track. Keep on this path for about a mile and a half until it meets a well used track at a stile. Turn right along the track, which can be muddy at times, past the old crossing keeper's cottage. Keep on the track for about a mile with Grimston Warren to your left and Roydon Common to your right. Go through a gate on the right signed "Roydon Common Footpath Only". Follow the path across the sandy common. At the far side turn right to the car park and keep on the firm track to the tarmac road.

3) Turn left along the road and about 150 yards later take the footpath on the right. Follow the path across the fields keeping a line of pine trees to your right. At the main A148 turn left and 150 yards on turn right into a "no-through road" which is the old line of the main road before the construction of the bypass and the Knight's Hill roundabout. Follow the old road as it bears left as far as a pair of cottages. Immediately before the first cottage turn right on to a grass path. Turn left around the cottage garden and keep on the path as far as the A149. Cross the main road and take the footpath opposite. At a minor road turn right and follow the road as far as the entrance to Rising Castle on the left. Enter the castle car park and a short distance later turn right into the castle's grounds. Work on the castle started about 1140 and it was modelled on the castle at Norwich. The vast earthworks that surround the castle cover 12 acres, making them among the largest earthworks of any castle in England. In 1331 the castle became the home, or prison depending on the extent of freedom she was allowed, of Queen Isabella, widow of Edward II. She was suspected of complicity in the murder of her husband by her lover Roger Mortimer. Her son, Edward III sent her to Castle Rising to keep her out of trouble until her death in 1358. Walk through the grounds with the castle to your left and leave by a gate. Cross the tarmac road and turn left along the pavement to the road junction. Cross the road and carry on ahead to the lychgate of the church. Go through the gate and cross the churchyard to leave by the gate opposite. The Alms Houses opposite were formally a leper colony and are occupied now by elderly ladies who attend the church attired in their cloaks and pointed hats. Much more could be said about Castle Rising and its history. As the old rhyme says: "Rising was a sea-port where Lynn was but a marsh. Now Lynn is a sea-port town, and Rising fares the worse".

11 – West Runton and Cromer

8¹/₂ Miles

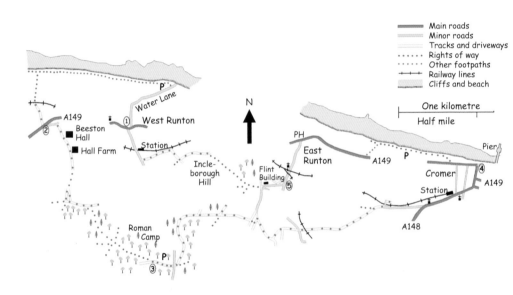

In places the North Norfolk Coastal Path is forced to leave the shoreline and divert inland to avoid crumbling cliffs. The length between West Runton and Cromer is notorious in this respect with great areas of the cliff tumbling into the sea each year. This may yield spectacular finds in the way of Giant Mammoth skeletons but it does render this area unsafe for walkers. The alternative route, adopted as the national trail, is in sharp contrast to the gentle stroll along the shore and takes the walker through wooded countryside up to the highest point in Norfolk! This walk starts in the centre of West Runton (OS Ref. 133/181427) which is readily accessible by train or bus. Car owners can pick up the route at the coastal car park just a short distance along Water Lane.

1) From the crossroads in the centre of the village walk along Water Lane to the beach car park. Turn left into the car park and walk along the edge of the grassy area keeping a safe distance from the cliff edge. After a mile, past the last of the caravan parks, turn left just before the assent of Beeston Bump. A post bearing the acorn logo of the National Trail indicates that this is now the official route of the North Norfolk Coastal Path. There are similar finger posts indicating the route at regular intervals between this point and Cromer; however some of the distances are inaccurate and so should generally be ignored. Follow the route over the railway crossing to the main road. Cross the road and turn left and then right into a small road leading to Beeston Hall.

2) Turn right to pass the Hall, now a school, and Hall Farm, and continue ahead uphill to meet a bridleway. At the Beeston Regis Heath National Trust sign turn left and a short distance later bear right at a fork by the West Runton National Trust sign. The path now enters woodland with a fairly steep climb along a sunken path. At the top of the hill turn left along a broad track leading to the Roman Camp car park. Local people introduced the name "Roman Camp" in the late 19th century although there is no evidence that the Romans ever inhabited the area. There are numerous humps and bumps to be found here but these are probably the

remains of old iron workings. This area, at 102 metres above sea level, is the highest point in Norfolk.

3) Walk through the car park and continue along the gravel road, keeping slightly left, to meet a tarmac road at Aylmerton. Cross over the road and carry on along the path ahead. Almost immediately bear left along a broad, uneven road leading to a caravan park. Pass the site entrance on the left and carry on along the tree-lined path. After a while the path leaves the woods and enters more open country. Cross a farm track and follow the signed path bearing right. Cross a tarmac road and go through the railway arch. On reaching the end of the gravel track cross the road and take the tarmac road straight ahead. At the main A148 turn left towards the town centre. Pass the supermarket and keep on straight ahead at the mini-roundabout. There are some interesting buildings here with attractive flint cottages on the left and a brick and flint chapel on the right. At the triangle in the centre of the town turn left, and follow the road to the seafront.

4) It is possible to drop down to the shore at this point and return to West Runton along the sand and shingle foreshore. However, this is dependent on the tides as well as the going underfoot and should only be attempted in good conditions. The inland return route is via the cliff car park towards the west and then on to the pavement alongside the A149 into East Runton. In the village centre turn left opposite the Fishing Boat pub and follow the road across the common and under the two railway bridges to the top common.

5) Turn right along the top common to a large, flint-built building on the corner of the road. As the road bears left keep straight ahead alongside the flint wall and carry on along this path. At a path junction go ahead keeping Incleborough Hill on your left. Half a mile later turn right at the entrance of the caravan site and follow the tarmac road across the golf course to Station Road. Turn right over the railway bridge to return to the starting point.

12 - East and West Rudham

8³/₄ Miles

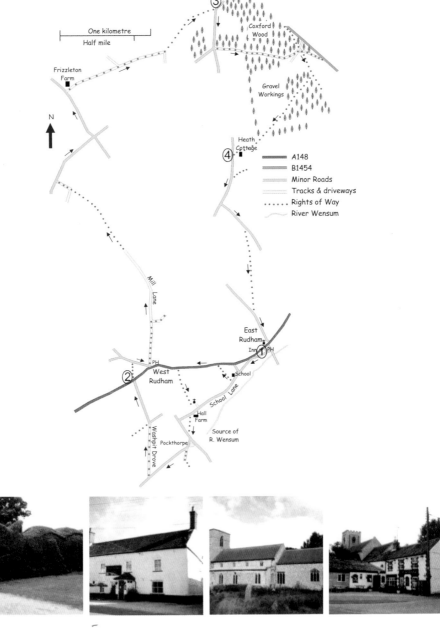

One kilometre
Half mile

Frizzleton Farm

Coxford Wood

Gravel Workings

N

Heath Cottage

③

④

A148
B1454
Minor Roads
Tracks & driveways
Rights of Way
River Wensum

Mill Lane

East Rudham
Inn ① PH
PH

West Rudham ②
PH
School

School Lane

Hall Farm

Washpit Drove
Pockthorpe

Source of R. Wensum

It can be frustrating to find that a planned walk falls on two adjacent Ordnance Survey (OS) sheets. For walkers in the Rudhams, this is heightened because most walks, including this one, require three of the Explorer Maps. The twin villages of East and West Rudham lie on the A148, midway between King's Lynn and Fakenham. The siting of three public houses on this stretch of the old road suggests that the villages were probably a staging post for travellers in the days of horse transport. Some years ago the Ramblers' Association held National Footpath Weeks with the objective of identifying and reopening problem footpaths. The route of this walk was chosen since most of the cross-field paths had not been reinstated and large sections were impassable. Today, thanks to the County Council Footpath Officers and the landowners, especially the Houghton Estate, the paths are all walkable. The walk starts at the triangle of grass in the centre of East Rudham (OS Ref. 132/825280), opposite the Crown Inn.

1) Cross the grass triangle in the direction of King's Lynn and, at the end of the Green, keep left along School Lane. About 100 yards past the school, take the footpath on the right. At the main road, cross over and turn left along the pavement. At the layby, cross over to the village green and take the footpath which is waymarked by a clump of trees. Follow the cross-field path, which for many years was impassable and not reinstated, to an iron gate leading into the churchyard. Walk through the churchyard back on to School Lane. West Rudham Church is no longer in regular use and is maintained by the Historic Churches Commission. Turn right and, a short distance past the farm, turn left to follow a cross-field path to Pockthorpe. At the road, turn left, and after a few yards turn right by a pond. The tiny village of Pockthorpe is unremarkable apart from being the source of the River Wensum that flows through Fakenham on its way to Norwich. Stay on the tarmac road as far as a concrete pad on the right. Take the path on the right between hedges and follow this old track, Washpit Drove, until it meets another tarmac road.

Carry on straight ahead along the road as far as the main A148.

2) Cross the busy road and follow the field-edge path opposite to the next minor road. Turn right along the road and left along the gravel track, Mill Lane. As you walk along the lane, look through gaps in the hedge on the left for views of Houghton Hall. It is said that Sir Robert Walpole created this vista to impress his brother-in-law Viscount Townshend at nearby Raynham Hall. Keep on straight ahead through woods and along field edges to the next tarmac road. Turn right along the road and left at the crossroads. At Frizzleton Farm, turn right through the farmyard. On your left, note the ornate hedge of one of the farm cottages cut in the shape of a giant dragon. Follow the farm track across several fields to a clump of trees on the left. Bear left along the diagonal cross-field path to a small copse on the far side. Turn right along the edge of the copse and then cross a small field to a tarmac road.

3) Turn right along the road and, in about a quarter of a mile, turn left along a gravel bridleway alongside Coxford Wood. The path goes downhill and, at the bottom of the slope, meets a broad track by a grass and wooded triangle. Cross over the broad track, servicing the gravel workings, and take the signed footpath through a wooden gate on the right. Take the first turning on the right through pine trees. To the right a high bank shields the huge gravel workings. Keep on this slightly uphill path to the road alongside Keeper's Cottage on the OS map or Heath Cottage on the house sign.

4) Turn left along the road and then left at the T-junction. After about 250 yards, go through a waymarked gap in the hedge on the right. Follow the path diagonally across the field to the left, heading towards the flagpole of East Rudham Church. The path leaves the field by a pair of houses and joins the road. Turn left along the road back to the A148 by the Cat and Fiddle pub. Turn right along the road to return to the start.

13 - Burnham Thorpe and Captain Wooget

9 Miles

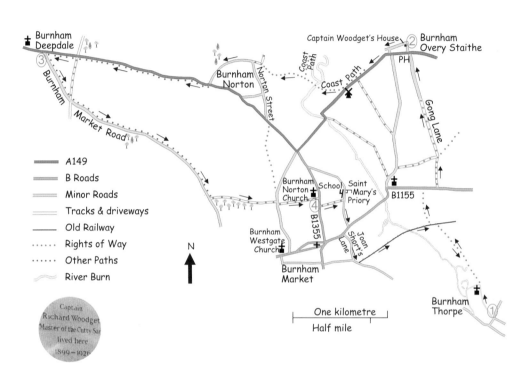

Burnham Deepdale

Captain Woodget's House

Burnham Overy Staithe

Burnham Norton

Coast Path

Coast Path

PH

Burnham Market Road

Gong Lane

A149

B Roads

Minor Roads

Tracks & driveways

Old Railway

Rights of Way

Other Paths

River Burn

Norton Street

Burnham Norton Church

School

Saint Mary's Priory

B1155

Burnham Westgate Church

B1355

Joan Short's Lane

Burnham Market

N

Captain Richard Woodget Master of the Cutty Sark lived here 1899 – 1926

One kilometre

Half mile

Burnham Thorpe

In 1885 Richard Woodget was appointed Captain of the Cutty Sark. In 1883 the ship, under its then Captain, sailed from Newcastle, New South Wales, to London in just 83 days beating every ship sailing at about the same time by 25 days to over a month. On Woodget's first voyage in command, the ship sailed from England to Sydney in 77 days and returned to the UK in 73 days. This was the start of 10 years of domination by Cutty Sark in the wool trade. This walk passes Captain Woodget's House at Burnham Overy Staithe and his burial place at Burnham Norton. The walk starts at Burnham Thorpe Village Hall (OS Ref. 132/854415)

1) From the village hall walk along the road heading north to Burnham Thorpe Church. Where the path turns left go through the kissing gate straight ahead and follow the path along the field edge to a series of large gates. Once through the gates head half left over a stream and then head for a kissing gate in the far hedge about two thirds of the way from the right corner. Go through the gate and turn left along an old railway line. In a short distance turn right off the railway into a field and follow the path along the right of the fields as far as the B1155. Turn right along the road and then left immediately after the last house into Gong Lane. Follow Gong Lane to meet the A149 by "The Hero" pub. Cross the road and carry on ahead along East Harbour Way. The last house on the left bears an inscription indicating that this was the home of Captain Woodget.

2) Turn left along the shore and follow the road around to rejoin the A149, turn right then right again at the end of the built up area following the acorn signs of the Coast Path. The path follows the line of the road inside the hedge then, at a point opposite the windmill, turns half right, crossing the field towards the marshes. Follow the acorn signs until the Coastal Path turns sharp right on a raised bank, then leave it to go ahead towards Burnham Norton Village. Where Norton Street joins from the left keep ahead along the tarmac road to again meet the A149. Cross the road and go through a hole in the hedge onto a field edge path. Turn

right along the path and follow it to Burnham Deepdale.

3) The path turns back sharp left by a house on the corner of the road. Carry on along this field edge path now following the Burnham Market Road. After about a mile and a quarter the path runs out at a wood. Turn left along a track through the wood. At a minor road turn right and almost immediately left along another track which leads to Burnham Norton Church. Enter the Churchyard by an iron gate on the left and turn left again. Towards the far left corner of the yard is the gravestone of Captain Woodget. The grave is easily recognised as it is covered by a large marble anchor. The inscription records his birth on 21 November 1846 and death on 5 March 1928. Nearby are older tombstones from the Woodgett family, presumably his parents who used a variant of the spelling. These indicate that he was very much a local boy. The round tower church is well worth a visit before continuing the walk.

4) From the church turn right along the B1355 heading towards Burnham Market and in a short distance turn left along a narrow footpath to a school. At the tarmac road the route is to the right (but a quick detour to the left are the ruins of Saint Mary's Carmelite Priory) Walk down the hill to the B1155 at Burnham Market. Turn right along the main road and in a hundred yards turn left along Joan Short's Lane. At a T-junction turn left along a concrete track to the left of a bungalow. Follow this disused railway line to rejoin the outward route by the kissing gate on the right and retrace the route across the field to the church and the start.

14 - Burnham Thorpe and Nelson

9¹/₂ Miles

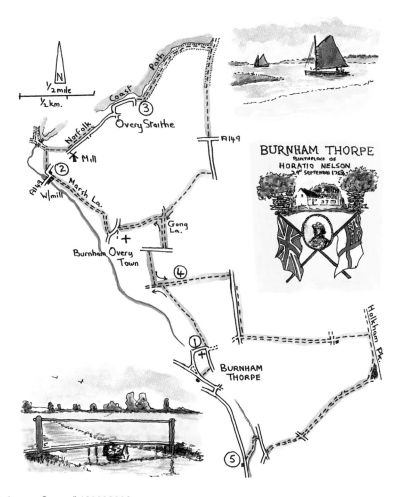

This walk is split into two parts. The first section, to the north, follows paths that Nelson may have taken as a boy, and lead to the coast. The latter segment, to the east and south, uses paths that he would have followed during his years "on the beach". Nelson had to visit Holkham Hall to get his pay application endorsed by the JP, Thomas William Coke, Lord Leicester. The walk includes most of the places of interest in the local area and, with the exception of a short length of disused railway line, uses paths that have changed little over the past 200 years. The walk starts at Burnham Thorpe Church (OS Ref 132/842418). For a shorter walk each section may be followed separately with suitable breaks at The Hero pub at Burnham Overy Staithe or the Lord Nelson at Burnham Thorpe.

1) From the car park to the north of the church go into the water meadow to the north of the graveyard via a kissing gate. Go through a cattle pen and follow the path diagonally to the left to another kissing gate in the far hedge. Turn left along the old railway line and, a short distance later, turn right along a field edge path and follow this to the tarmac road in Burnham Overy Town. Cross the road, and turn right along the pavement. Shortly after the pavement runs out, turn left along the track called "Gong Lane". At the cross path, turn left along a grass track and follow this to the road by Burnham Overy Church. Strangely, although Nelson's father was rector of Burnham Thorpe Church and several more of the Burnham churches, he was not rector of the Overy Town Church. This fell to the rector of Burnham Westgate, and now is the principal church of Burnham Market. Turn left along the road and, a short distance later, turn right sharply along a green lane – Marsh Lane. Go through a gate alongside Burnham Overy Watermill and, at the main A149 road, carry on straight ahead.

2) At the bend in the road take the path on the left through a field, keeping the hedge to the right. Cross a stile and turn right along the North Norfolk Coastal Path. The Coastal Path crosses a field, giving a fine view of a well-restored windmill. Follow the path alongside the main road on to the pavement, and then turn left into Burnham Overy Staithe. Staithe is Middle English for "strand" or "coal wharf" and it is recorded that during the five years from 1787 onwards Nelson often walked here and read his newspaper, hoping to find news that would lead to his recall to active service. Where the tarmac road turns away from the coast, keep straight ahead on to the grass and gravel path.

3 Keep on the Coastal Path as it bends around to the right. Where the path bends to the left take the gated track on the right, and follow this through a series of gates on to the main road. Cross the road and continue ahead on the minor road for nearly a quarter of a mile then turn right along the waymarked path. Follow the waymarks across the fields to rejoin the outward route at Gong Lane. Return to the disused railtrack and keep going along the track past the gate used on the outward journey.

4) Keep on the disused rail track, now a conservation walk, and follow the signs across two footbridges into an orchard. Keep alongside the hedge of the orchard on to the tarmac road. Turn right and, a short distance later, enter a field through a gap on the left then turn right immediately to follow the field edge path with the hedge to the right. At a cross track turn left, and follow this stony track, past some fine brick barns, to the perimeter wall of Holkham Hall. As Nelson walked along this path on his way to Holkham Hall he was very aware of the poor conditions of the farm workers toiling in the fields. He was so distressed by the poverty he found there that he wrote to his friend, Prince William, the Duke of Clarence, pleading for some improvement in their situation. At that time a man's earnings for the year would be £23 1s 0d whilst Nelson, on half pay, was earning £146 plus £100 a year from his uncle and £100 a year for his wife Fanny from her uncle. At the wall turn right along an old Roman road. At the junction take the right fork and, at the end of the small copse, turn right along a farm track. Follow this track, crossing over the first tarmac road, and after about a mile, turn right along the road at the end of the track. A short distance beyond this, go through a gap in the hedge on the left just before a cattle pen. Turn right in the water meadows and follow the line of hedge on the right to cross the River Burn by a footbridge. Turn left and follow the river bank to a stile, close to the site of Nelson's birthplace.

5) Nelson was born on September 29, 1758 at the parsonage that stood on this site. The house has been demolished since to make way for a much grander building, and now the site is remembered by a plaque on the wall alongside the road. From the plaque, turn north along the road towards Burnham Thorpe. About half a mile later, opposite the Creake Road sign, turn right, and at the next road junction turn left towards the village centre. At the Lord Nelson Public House, known as "The Plough" in Nelson's days, cross the village green on the right and turn left along the road back to the church.

15 - Hilgay and The Wissey

11 Miles

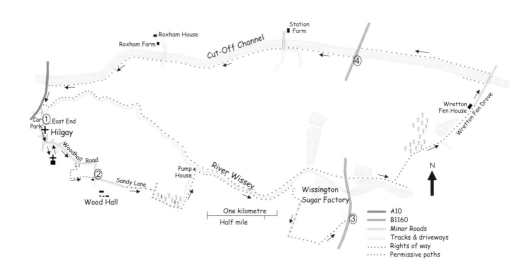

Roxham House
Roxham Farm
Station Farm
Cut-Off Channel
④
Wretton Fen House
Wretton Fen Drove
Car Park ① East End
Hilgay
Woodhall Road
Pump House
River Wissey
N
② Sandy Lane
Wood Hall
Wissington Sugar Factory
One kilometre
Half mile
③

A10
B1160
Minor Roads
Tracks & driveways
Rights of way
Permissive paths

For a number of years it has been impossible to use the public footpath along the south side of the River Wissey which passed through the Wissington Sugar Factory. Recently the owners of the sugar factory have applied for, and obtained, a diversion of the public right of way. The diversion now takes walkers around the factory following a new path. Although this walk is 11 miles, it follows the River Wissey or the Cut-off Channel all the way so there are no hills to climb. It is also very easy to cut the walk short by turning around at the factory and returning along the north bank of the river. The walk starts by the Bridge Street bus stop in the centre of Hilgay opposite the road marked "East End" (OS Ref. 143/621987).

1) Walk along Bridge Street away from the river passing the Hilgay Methodist Chapel on the left. At the village sign turn left towards Stocks Hill (why will you find a cannon and a sailing boat on the village sign? Read on to find out more...). At the road junction turn right along Lawrence's Lane and left at the major road to arrive at the lychgate of the parish church. Walk down the tree-lined avenue to the church and at the church building walk anticlockwise to a point on the far side a few yards short of the west end. Here, close to the wall, is a tombstone which reads: "Here lies the body of George William Manby Captain Royal Navy, born 1766, died 1854, inventor of an apparatus for saving life in shipwrecks. Grant him Lord eternal rest." This solves the earlier question about the village sign. What Captain Manby invented was the rocket-propelled line fired on to shipwrecks that would then carry the breeches buoy to bring the crew back to land. Return to the road and carry on along Woodhall Road. At a bend, by some large oaks, turn right and follow the footpath sign. The path goes around three sides of a field and back to the road by the entrance of Wood Hall. This was the home of Captain Manby.

2) Carry on along the road leaving the hall entrance to the right. At a road junction bear right and then left. Pass the edge of a wood and immediately after crossing a small drain turn left along a grass path heading towards an old pumping station on the riverbank. Turn right at the pump house and follow the bank of the River Wissey towards the sugar factory.

After a bend in the river the waymarked path leaves the bank and is diverted around the south side of the factory. At a hard track turn right and follow the track, past a heap of bog oak, to a field edge path on the left (bog oak is found throughout the dark fen soil - the large trunks of the trees have been preserved in the acid peat and these become a hazard to agricultural machinery). Follow the field edge path to a footbridge by the sugar factory's main gate.

3) Wissington Sugar Factory is among the largest sugar factories in Europe. Originally the sugar beet industry was started up after the first world war to ensure that the country was not totally reliant on cane sugar imported from Cuba and other countries. Now that the cheap food policy is in operation the subsidy paid for beet has been reduced and so in order to maintain profitability the factory has diversified. Nowadays it uses waste heat and carbon dioxide to heat glasshouses for tomatoes, and is currently constructing plant to turn sugar into biofuel. At the main road turn left and cross over the Wissey. Turn right at the footpath sign (or turn left to return to Hilgay on the shorter route) and a few yards later on keep left on the path towards the river. Follow the riverbank for nearly half a mile to a wooden footbridge on the left, then follow the path across open fields to some scrubby woods. At a fork in the path keep left. Pass through the front of a large house and carry on along the road to the Cut-off Channel. The Cut-off Channel is a man-made channel which takes surplus water from the River Ouse at Denver and delivers it into the water-starved areas of Essex. Cross the bridge and immediately turn left along the path. Keep on the path as far as the next bridge. Cross the bridge to the south side of the channel and turn right to continue alongside the channel.

4) The walk continues along the south side of the channel all the way to the A10 at Hilgay. The change in direction is after about one-and-a-half miles, at the Roxham Farm crossing, when it is advisable to leave the grass bank and walk along the gravel path a few yards further away from the channel. At the A10 turn left along the busy main road and then left, over the bridge, to return to the start.

16 – Stody Estate Walk

12 Miles

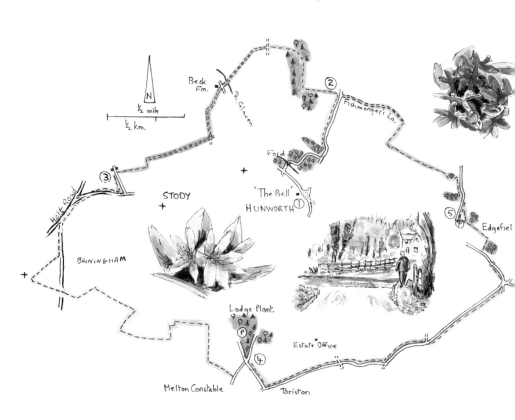

The Stody Estate lies between Melton Constable and Holt. It is known as being at the forefront of agricultural practice, at the forefront in encouraging managed public access, and for the 10 acres of rhododendrons and azaleas on display at the open days in May each year. For walkers, the nine mile circuit of the estate, almost entirely on Countryside Stewardship paths, is an example of how landowners can encourage responsible access. The route is well signed with arrows showing the path and clear No Entry signs to prevent unauthorised access that could interfere with the farming and other activities of the estate. This walk extends the route to 12 miles by starting and finishing at the Bell Inn at Hunworth (OS Ref 133/070352). Because the route is almost entirely on paths which do not appear on the OS maps, walkers are advised to download a map from the Stody Estate's website: *www.stodyestate.co.uk*.

1) The landlord of the Bell at Hunworth has given permission for ramblers to use the car park at the rear of the Inn on the understanding that many of them will use the facilities before or after the walk. To start the walk, leave the car park and turn left alongside a grass triangle. Keep on along King Street signposted to Stody and Thornage. Pass some attractive flint cottages on the right and just under half a mile from the Inn turn right at a crossroads. The road is narrow with a poorly maintained surface. A short distance later cross the River Glaven by a footbridge alongside a ford. Keep on the road through the wood as far as the tarmac road. At this point there are two alternatives. Either turn left along the busy road with no footway, or turn sharp left for a few yards and then clamber up a steep bank into the woods on the right. Both alternatives will join up with a field edge path on the left of the road at the top of the hill. Take this path and follow it to the end of the field where it meets the circular route around the estate.

2) Turn left along the field headland. From this point there is a general instruction to follow the waymarked path around the estate to return eventually to this point. The route goes through woods into open fields. It crosses the disused railway line that once connected Melton Constable with Holt, and continues along what is now called the Poppy Line to Sheringham. At Beck Farm cross the river and the road and continue straight ahead through the farmyard, keeping the buildings to the right. The route follows a public bridleway for about 500 yards and then leaves the bridleway where it meets the old railway track once more. Turn right on to a grass path with the track in a cutting to the left. To the left is the round, flint tower of Stody Church. Where the track runs out follow the signs along a field edge path to a tarmac road.

3) Cross the road into a field and follow the grass headland left and right. Towards the end of the field follow the signs taking the path across the road and continue in the same direction along the opposite field edge. By the Burgh Stubbs road junction cross the road and turn left along the field edge. At a small copse the path bears right away from the road and follows a ditch to a bridge on the left. Carry on in the same direction on the opposite side of the ditch. Briningham Church can just be seen in the woods ahead. The path now bears sharp left along a field edge as far as the road. Cross the road and follow the field edge turning left at the field corner onto a grass path. Cross the bridge on the right and then left and right to a footpath heading towards Melton Constable. Turn right along the footpath and shortly follow waymarks to the right around field edges to the Stody road.

4) Cross the road and continue along the road opposite towards the Stody Estate offices. A short while later turn left through a gap into a field and follow the field edge paths alongside the road for about two miles to Edgefield. This is a predominately arable area with the usual crops of cereals and sugar beet plus some less usual crops such as carrots and daffodils. At Edgefield the path follows the road to the left and eventually it is necessary to leave the grass paths and join the tarmac road for a short distance. Take the permissive path on the right, bear right inside the gate and almost immediately left along the headland path. Go through a gate and turn left across a grass field to the alternative car park. The tower of Edgefield Church can be seen in a wooded area nearby.

5) At the car park turn right along the field edge to a gate in the corner of the field. Cross the road and pick up the route in the copse opposite. Follow the signs around the edge of the large refuse pit. Cross the stream and follow the route along Fishmonger's Lane back to point ② Return to the starting point by turning left and reversing the outward journey.

The Ramblers' have over 50 Areas and over 400 Local Groups.
All are actively involved in providing a full and varied walks programme for
local members and in the work of monitoring, maintaining and improving
the local Rights of Way network, and preserving the beauty of the
Countryside.

For details of membership of the Ramblers' contact: -
THE RAMBLERS', 2nd FLOOR, CAMELFORD HOUSE,
87-90 ALBERT EMBANKMENT, LONDON SE1 7TW.
020 7339 8500.

Price £3.30

ISBN 978-1-906494-18-6

9 781906 494186 >

ramblers
at the heart of walking

Printed by clanpress, 01553 772737